CW00501902

r/88

£2

AC/FORD/SHELBY
COBRA
Rod Grainger

CONTENTS

Foulis

Haynes

ISBN 0 85429 381 7

A FOULIS Motoring Book

First published 1984

© **Haynes Publishing Group**

All rights reserved. No part of this book may be reproduced or transmitted in any form or by any means, electronic or mechanical, including photocopying, recording or by any information storage or retrieval system, without written permission from the publisher.

Published by:
Haynes Publishing Group
Sparkford, Yeovil,
Somerset BA22 7JJ

Distributed in USA by:
Haynes Publications Inc.
861 Lawrence Drive, Newbury Park,
California 91320, USA

Dust jacket design: Rowland Smith
Jacket colour illustration: The AC-Shelby-Cobra 289 Mk II, chassis number COB6029, of John Haynes, photographed by Les Brazier
Page Layout: Mike King
Photographs: Andrew Morland, Les Brazier, L.A.T, John McLellan and Rod Leach.
Road tests: Courtesy of Motor and Autosport
Printed in England by: J.H.Haynes & Co. Ltd

Titles in the *Super Profile* series

Ariel Square Four (F388)
BMW R69 & R69S (F387)
BSA Bantam (F333)
Honda CB750 sohc (F351)
MV Agusta America (F334)
Norton Commando (F335)
Sunbeam S7 & S8 (F363)
Triumph Thunderbird (F353)
Triumph Trident (F352)

Austin-Healey 'Frogeye' Sprite (F343)
Chevrolet Corvette (F432)
Ferrari 250GTO (F308)
Fiat X1/9 (F341)
Ford Cortina 1600E (F310)
Ford GT40 (F332)
Jaguar E-Type (F370)
Jaguar D-Type & XKSS (F371)
Jaguar Mk 2 Saloons (F307)
Jaguar SS90 & SS100 (F372)
Lancia Stratos (F340)
Lotus Elan (F330)
Lotus Seven (F385)
MGB (F305)
MG Midget & Austin-Healey Sprite (except 'Frogeye') (F344)
Morris Minor Series MM (F412)
Morris Minor & 1000 (ohv) (F331)
Porsche 911 Carrera (F311)
Rolls-Royce Corniche (F411)
Triumph Stag (F342)

B29 Superfortress (F339)
Boeing 707 (F356)
Harrier (F357)

Mosquito (F422)
Phantom II (F376)
P51 Mustang (F423)
Sea King (F377)
Super Etendard (F378)
Tiger Moth (F421)

Great Western Kings (F426)
Intercity 125 (F428)
V2 'Green Arrow' Class (F427)

Further titles in this series will be published at regular intervals. For information on new titles please contact your bookseller or write to the publisher.

FOREWORD

The Cobra was, and is, a phenomenon. The mating of the elegant and simple AC Ace body to the brutal power and stump-pulling torque of a large capacity American V8 engine was an inspiration, even if not a new idea, for Sydney Allard certainly got there first.

Automotive history is littered with other people's attempts to create similar packages – Sunbeam Tiger, Daimler SP250 (Dart), MGB V8, TR7 V8, etc – but none has succeeded as brilliantly as the Cobra. Simply, the Cobra was greater than the sum of its parts.

Undoubtedly some of the Cobra myth was created by the hyperbole which is inevitably associated with Carroll Shelby: a showman of the first order, who has not only the ability to pluck publicity from thin air, but also the charm to talk into an alliance such disparate entities as the AC Car Company and the giant Ford Motor Company – with Shelby American in the centre. Nevertheless, the Cobra was always a car which surprised and inspired those lucky enough to drive it. In Richard J. Kopec's *Shelby American Guide* a stationary Cobra is described as a hand grenade waiting for the pin to be pulled – and I guess that just about sums up the Cobra's character.

Shelby's presence always looms so large in the Cobra story that the very real amount of time and effort put into the car's development by both AC and Ford is often overlooked. Somehow, when the car did well it was always a Shelby Cobra but when it had problems it became an AC or Ford. This must have been particularly hard for FoMoCo to swallow as they backed the 'Ford Cobra' with hard cash in the hope that the performance image would rub off on their products. Some of it did off course, but most of the glory went to Shelby. Hence Ford's pulling the plug on the Cobra in favour of the GT40.

I enjoyed writing this book for, like most enthusiasts bored with the emasculated sports cars of today, I would love to have a Cobra in my garage. I hope like-minded readers will enjoy the Cobra's story.

I would like to offer my sincere thanks to AC Cars Ltd, John McLellan and Rod Leach – without their help the compilation of this book would have been almost impossible.

Rod Grainger

HISTORY & EVOLUTION

In retrospect the formula for the Cobra seems so simple – refined European chassis, big strong American V8 – that its inception and production seem to have been inevitable. In truth, however, had the dice of fate fallen just a little differently, the car might easily never have existed. It took a large measure of serendipity for the paths of a tall, wiry ex-professional racing driver Texan and a small British traditional sports car manufacturer to cross at exactly the right time. But cross they did and, as a result, our motoring heritage is much richer.

Carroll Shelby

Carroll Shelby was born on January 11th, 1923, in the small town of Leesburg which is just over 100 miles north-east of Dallas, Texas. Carroll's father was a country postman who, in the early twenties, was still making his deliveries by horse and buggy. It would not be long, however, before Shelby senior was equipped with a car for his daily work, and often accompanied by the young Carroll – whose fascination by things automotive soon became evident.

Carroll's upbringing was as normal as could have been expected through the years of depression which afflicted the world of that time. After high school, Carroll Shelby joined the US Army Air Corps and by 1942 was a sergeant and flying instructor. Married in 1943, he left the Army in 1945 having never seen active service.

There followed a period of partnership in a road haulage company, and a stint in the oil fields of Texas. However, Carroll, who now had two children to support, was only just making ends meet and therefore decided that his fortune would be made in the factory-farming of chickens. He invested every penny he had in this project – as well as many pennies he didn't have – only to see the project wiped out when he lost his entire stock of birds to disease. Carroll was bankrupt, and not yet thirty!

'It's an ill-wind ...' This disaster threw Carroll into semi-professional motor racing in order to scrape a living. His natural ability shone through and he was soon seen as a world-class sports racing car driver. Drives in Allards, Aston Martins, Maseratis and Ferraris took him to a level of ability sufficient to win Le Mans (with Roy Salvadori) in 1959, driving an Aston Martin DBR1.

With a reputation probably much larger than his bank balance, in 1961 Carroll Shelby started a school for would-be-racing drivers based at the Riverside track in California. The school was a success immediately, enabling Carroll to take on his first employee, Pete Brock, as a driving instructor and general assistant. Pete Brock, who had previously worked for Chevrolet and who had been much involved in the 'Stingray' project, was to play a very important role in the Cobra story.

AC and the Ace/Aceca

AC was a company with a long history who, in the fifties, were producing a traditional British sports car called the 'Ace'. Introduced at the 1953 Earls Court Motor Show in prototype form, with barchetta styling very similar to contemporary Ferraris, the Ace was in production by early 1954. The original production models were fitted with AC's own straight-six engine giving around 105bhp. The Ace's hand-built chassis, originally designed by John Tojeiro, featured two 3-inch diameter longitudinal tubes joined ladder-fashion by small diameter cross-pieces and both ends of the chassis had turrets to carry transverse leaf springs. From this base rose a tubular semi-spaceframe to give more rigidity to the basic chassis and to carry the hand-fashioned alloy panels which formed the shapely body. The resulting car has a dry weight of just 15cwt, giving a very respectable power to weight ratio for a sports two-seater of its time. Independent suspension endowed the machine with excellent handling.

In the fifties, however, sports car development was moving apace and by the mid-fifties the Ace's performance was beginning to pale against the offerings from other factories; simply, the car was underpowered. But what could the tiny AC company of Thames Ditton do? They knew that their own 2-litre engine was not capable of further development, so what was the solution?

For many years, Bristol had been making a 2-litre straight-six engine under licence from BMW – in fact it was derived from the famous 328 unit with its hemi-combustion chambers and unusual cross-over valve actuating mechanism – and using it in cars of their own manufacture, which also bore a strong resemblance to certain BMW designs. The Bristol

5

engine gave an easy 120bhp – more with some simple tuning-and was available to AC as Bristol had excess engine manufacturing capacity. Thus, from early in 1956, the Ace and Aceca (a coupé based on the Ace) became available with the Bristol engine.

Unfortunately for AC – or so it must have seemed at the time – changes within the Bristol company in the late fifties meant that it was no longer possible to produce the engine which the Ace used. Starved of their normal power unit, AC fell back on the Ford Zephyr saloon straight-six engine – but it was not the same, sales fell and the writing seemed to be on the wall for the Ace.

The Big Idea

Carroll Shelby, used to both American and European competition cars, appreciated the different philosophy behind each type of machine. Basically American racing and road sports cars relied upon brute horsepower to compensate for crude chassis, whilst European cars of the same genre had such good handling that they only needed small power units to achieve high average speeds. Shelby reasoned that the marriage of easy power with fine handling would produce something really rather special. Maybe the Allards he had driven during his racing career created this idea – who knows? But it was not a new idea for Shelby because, as he recollects in *The Cobra Story*, he had approached Jensen, Aston Martin, Maserati and de Tomaso with his concept in the mid-fifties – to no avail.

Shelby would have known of AC and the Ace because of his drives for European factories, particularly Aston Martin. During 1961, therefore, when news reached him of AC's engine problems he probably realised immediately that here, literally, was

the ideal vehicle for his idea of a trans-Atlantic mechanical marriage.

Carroll Shelby wasted no time in sending a letter to the Hurlocks (AC was their family business) outlining his ideas, although at the time he had no idea which American engine would be most suitable and did not even know about the forthcoming lightweight V8 from Ford. AC did not dismiss the idea out of hand, and, as luck would have it, Shelby heard about the new Ford V8 in the autumn. This engine was cast in iron by a new thinwall process making it almost as light as an alloy unit, but with none of the problems associated with that material. It was intended for use in the Ford Fairlane.

Thinking that this new unit sounded ideal for his personal project, Shelby contacted a recent acquaintance, Dave Evans, of the Ford Motor Company, to explain his ideas. Evans was obviously enthusiastic as two of the 221 cubic inch engines were almost immediately despatched to Dean Moon's speedshop in Santa Fe Springs for evaluation by Shelby. (Shelby was sharing these premises as the base for a Goodyear distributorship and Champion franchise; both of which he was operating in addition to his racing school.)

The Ford engine proved almost bullet-proof under testing and very tunable. Dimensions, weight and power output were sent to England so that AC could assess the problems which would have to be overcome in fitting this unit to the Ace – they turned out to be relatively minor.

Armed with this knowledge, Shelby flew to England to finalise the deal and therefore clear the way for a prototype. About this time a 260cid version of the Ford V8 became available and, deemed even more suitable for his project than the 221, an example was despatched to AC in Thames Ditton for trial fitting in the prototype they were constructing. Shelby was able

to spend a considerable amount of time in the UK to assist in the building of the prototype and was rewarded, in January 1962, by being able to test drive the car on the Silverstone circuit. The car was everything he had expected: it was outrageously accelerative and fast, handled predictably (if driven with firmness) and had excellent braking. The machine, like any prototype, needed detail development but was basically a sound package – remarkably so when it is considered that the prototype's chassis was in fact very little altered from that of the Ace. It had been necessary to beef-up a few brackets and substitute an American Ford gearbox as the AC item simply couldn't take 260bhp and its associated torque. Luckily, the V8 at around 500lb was only a few pounds heavier than the standard Bristol engine so the overall balance of the car was barely affected. (Involuntary R&D testing by Shelby's early customers would bring more problems to light, but more of that later ...)

The prototype was numbered 'CSX0001' according to Carroll Shelby and 'CSX2000' according to the Shelby American Automobile Club. Similarly, according to Shelby 'CSX' stood for 'Carroll Shelby Experimental' and according to AC for 'Carroll Shelby Export'. The author is inclined to believe the latter in both cases. Whatever its true number the prototype was shipped to Santa Fe, *sans* engine which AC retained.

It is a part of motoring folklore that Shelby dreamed-up the 'Cobra' name one night and jotted it on a pad by his bedside. Whether the story is true or not, by the time the prototype arrived in the States, Pete Brock had already designed the, now famous, Cobra badge – it transpired that there were a few trademark problems with this name, but all were eventually overcome.

The unpainted prototype arrived in Santa Fe late in February 1962. Shelby enthusiasm ensured that the car was fitted with an engine and was running before the end of the day on which it arrived! The priority then was for Dave Evans of Ford to evaluate the car as soon as possible – Shelby knew the whole project had no real credibility without Ford's backing in the supply of engines.

The Shelby luck held out. Ford liked the car and could obviously see its potential for promoting the Ford name and for enlivening their rather stodgy image. Nevertheless, Shelby must have done some smooth talking with the Ford executives for, not only were they prepared to supply him with engines, but they would do so on credit! Additionally, Ford would allow Cobras to be sold through Ford dealerships throughout the USA and Shelby was invited to show the car as part of Ford's exhibit at the spring New York Auto Show.

With the Ford deal buttoned-up, Carroll Shelby, with some more fast talking, was able to reach agreement with AC, who also would supply their product on credit. Shelby was in business!

Production

Journalists lucky enough to test the prototype loved it, warts and all, and made no bones about saying so in their copy. The Cobra was also the sensation of the New York Auto Show which generated many firm orders backed by cash. And Shelby didn't have to worry about approaching Ford dealers – they were approaching him!

Against this background Shelby had been able to place a firm order with AC for 100 body/chassis units – the minimum quantity needed to homologate the new car in the FIA GT racing class.

By June 1962 the first 30 production cars had been completed and business was so

good that Dean Moon's premises were no longer adequate, but, with Ford's backing, Shelby was able to acquire the ex-Lance Reventlow premises in Venice, California – this is where the well-known Scarab sports racing cars had been built.

In truth, particularly in the earliest days, when the first 30 cars were built, there was really no such thing as a standard Cobra. There were two reasons for this:
1) customers could choose a specification for their car dependent upon how they intended to use it – a practice which would be continued in the future;
2) customer feedback and AC's/Shelby's own testing results created a programme which amounted to continuous modification, some of the modifications even being made retrospectively. In this period attention was given to axle ratios, front hubs and spindles, suspension geometry, cockpit ventilation and engine modifications. There were also a number of bodywork refinements.

During 1962 a steady trickle of Cobra chassis crossed the Atlantic by ship, destined for Venice, California – after all AC built each chassis/body unit by hand in the traditional manner and were hard pushed to complete more than ten to fifteen Cobras a week. Nevertheless, as the year progressed the tantalising FIA target of 100 cars for homologation drew ever closer. But major changes were afoot.

The 289cid V8 becomes available

Ford had been working on the 260cid engine and now had available a 289cid development which, in high performance guise, offered 271bhp. Shelby American very quickly acquired the right to use this engine in the Cobra, and

from the 76th car onward it became the Cobra's standard power plant. In Cobra trim this V8 came with solid tappets and a high-lift camshaft. Incidentally, AC called their version of this car the 'AC-Shelby-Cobra 289' whilst Carroll Shelby called his the 'Shelby-AC-Cobra'.

Towards the end of 1962 Carroll Shelby was itching to test the Cobra in serious motorsport, and a golden opportunity to do just that arose in October.

The SCCA (Sports Car Club of America) were running a three-hour endurance race as a support feature for the Times Grand Prix at Riverside Raceway, California. This particular endurance race included an experimental class for the benefit of the new 327cid-engined Corvette – a car which was not yet homologated under SCCA rules and therefore not eligible for the GT class and the associated Championship points. It did not take Shelby long to cotton on: if GM could do it, so could he! A liberal dose of the Shelby charm administered to the SCCA saw Bill Krause sitting on the startline, amongst the Corvettes, in Cobra CSX2002 which bore the racing number 'XP 98'.

CSX2002 was, of course, the second Cobra built and as such was fitted with the 260cid engine – although this particular unit had been blueprinted (carefully assembled and with optimum tolerances throughout) as this car was being used as a development 'mule' by Shelby American. Other changes from standard specification were minor – a flyscreen and rollbar had been fitted, and the radiator grille removed.

The little Cobra was dynamite! It showed a clean pair of tail lights to the Corvettes and had a lead of almost 1.5 miles after an hour's racing when disaster struck: a hub carrier shattered, proving the racers' adage: 'to finish first, you first have to finish'.

The requisite 100 Cobras

were completed in time for the FIA to grant official homologation to the model for the GT category of the 1963 racing season. Shortly afterwards a welcome change of specification arrived with the adoption of rack and pinion steering for the Cobra, in place of the inevitably vague worm and sector system previously used.

More or less concurrent with this change was the winding up of Bristol-engined Ace and Aceca production back at the Thames Ditton factory of AC.

Now that the Cobra qualified for international sports car racing in the GT class, Carroll Shelby was keen to have a crack at the greatest of all sports car races, Le Mans – a race he had himself won with Roy Salvadori in an Aston Martin DBR1 in 1959. To this end he commissioned AC to build two special Cobras to compete in the 1963 event – these cars featured an extended aluminium hardtop, giving them the general appearance of fastback coupés, special wheels and modified wheel arches. They also sported a set of cooling louvres in each front wing – a feature which apart from one short break would be standard on production cars from this time onwards. As a matter of interest, AC constructed a third Le Mans coupé-style car which has sold privately to a private customer in South Africa.

The two cars commissioned by Shelby American were entered for the Le Mans race of June 15th/16th, 1963; one by AC Cars Ltd, the other by American Shelby dealer Ed Hugus of Pittsburgh. As usual, with an endurance event of this length, attrition took a terrible toll on the 49 cars – including 11 Ferraris (!) – which started, only 13 reaching the finish. Amongst the DNFs was the Hugus car which, when running 13th just before halftime, suffered a blown engine. The other Cobra, driven by P. Bolton/N. Sanderson swept on to take 7th overall and 4th in the GT class at an average speed of 107.99 mph. It was preceded by 6

Ferraris ...

Shelby American ordered six Le Mans Replicas from AC, three of which were campaigned by the Shelby American team in the 1963 USRRC (United States Road Racing Championship) series. The other three cars were sold to American privateers to contest the SCCA A/Production series.

It was noticeable that the performance of the hard-topped coupé-style Cobras was better than its roadster counterpart – an improvement obviously brought about by better aerodynamics. This set off a chain of thought within the Shelby organisation which would eventually bear fruit in the form of the 'Daytona', a true coupé. More of this later.

Autumn of 1963 saw the advent of the Cobra 'Dragonsnake' – an off-the-shelf, but serious, drag racing car. Alternatively, you could buy the necessary parts from your local Shelby dealer to turn your street Cobra into a Dragonsnake. The latter system was much in line with Shelby thinking which allowed you to buy, from Shelby American, the components to turn your own Cobra into a competitive GT racer, hillclimber or sprinter – and goes a long way to explain why, in America at least, there are so few original Cobras (if there ever was such a thing anyway). You could have your Dragonsnake with the standard 271bhp or, if you preferred, with 300bhp, 325bhp or a massive 380bhp. Drag racing auto-transmissions and suitable rear axle ratios were also available.

In motorsport, 1963 had provided mixed fortunes for the Cobra. In America, in various forms and in many stages of tune, Cobras had won numerous SCCA races in the hands of privateers. In USRRC, the forerunner of CanAm, Cobras had swept the board in the latter part of the season and had won the series resoundingly. On the international scene, in FIA-recognised events, things looked somewhat bleak. The Le Mans story has already been related, and

mechanical problems dogged Shelby's Cobras at Daytona and Sebring. There was one bright spot, a very bright spot, when Dan Gurney was first past the chequered flag in a Cobra roadster at Bridgehampton – the very first time an American car had won an international race!

By the end of 1963 Shelby American had the benefit of much knowledge gained in the continuous development of their own team's competition cars, as well as seat-of-the-pants feedback from their private customers. This information was put to good use in formulating the specification of some very special roadsters ordered from AC with a serious onslaught of the 1964 FIA GT Championship in mind. At this point it should be explained that until the Le Mans Replicas previously mentioned, AC had only ever supplied Shelby American with standard rolling chassis/body units – all performance/handling modifications being carried out in Shelby's facility in Venice, California. The Replicas, however, which represented an interim stage in competition car development in terms of chassis and body modifications, had competition changes built in at Thames Ditton.

By January 1964, three of the FIA roadsters had arrived in California – each with bulbous flared wheel arches to cover the large Hallibrand alloy racing wheels, cut-outs below the radiator grille to feed air to the oil cooler and a revised bootlid giving enough room in the boot to carry the FIA's imaginary suitcase. The massive flaring of the rear wheel arches had been accommodated by shortening the doors from their standard length. These cars also featured heavy duty anti-roll bars, Koni dampers, revised steering links and various modifications to strengthen the chassis. Each was resplendent in blue paintwork with an identifying, contrasting stripe across the bonnet. Ultimately, five of these FIA Roadsters were built.

The Daytona coupé

In February 1964, one of the landmarks of Cobra history was reached when the Daytona coupé made its debut at the Daytona 12-Hour endurance race.

As stated earlier, Shelby had realised that a more aerodynamic shape was needed for the Cobra so that its engine power could be exploited to the full, and so that it could meet cars like the sleek Ferrari 250 GTO on more equal terms. Within the FIA rules, any body could be fitted to a homologated chassis as long as the chassis and the basic mechanical specification remained unchanged.

Shelby American took the bull by the horns. Starting with a clean sheet, and working from standard chassis dimensions, Pete Brock designed a new body to cover the Cobra's hardware. In California, a wooden buck was created on a spare chassis and this was in turn used to hand-fashion the alloy panels which would eventually clothe a bare chassis specially ordered from AC.

Despite the fact that the first Daytona coupé was created from sketches – there never was a proper blueprint – it achieved all its design targets. With a 385bhp 289cid engine it was capable of running to 180mph, with a 25 per cent fuel saving over the roadster! Brock put a great deal of thought, and experience, into his design even if in 1963/4 the application of aerodynamics was a black art. The snake's new skin was supported on a small-diameter tube spaceframe which had sprung from that bare AC chassis. The bodywork swept backwards from the car's low nose to a sharply raked windscreen, across a low, slightly convex, roof and then via a gently curved plexiglass rear window to the abruptly terminated tail panel. Airflow along the car's flanks was undisturbed, save for the large air extractors behind the side windows.

The Daytona also featured a flat bottom, facilitated by recessing the exhaust boxes into the sill panels.

After shakedown tests on the first Daytona, five further examples would be built during 1964 – but not in California. Five bare chassis were shipped to Shelby American by AC. These chassis received the same modifications as the first in America, before being shipped to *Carrozzeria* Gran Sport in Modena, Italy, where the alloy bodies would be fabricated. One can imagine the interest this must have generated amongst Gran Sport's well-known neighbours in that small Italian town!

Back to the Daytona race. Driven by Dave MacDonald and Bob Holbert, the blue Daytona coupé, bearing race number 14, immediately showed that it had the legs on the Ferrari GTOs, and was five laps in the lead when it pulled into the pits two-thirds of the way through the race. Then disaster struck. A pit fire during refuelling put the car out of action – luckily no one was seriously hurt and the car was saveable. In fact the car was rebuilt in time for the following month's Sebring race where it crossed the finishing line first in class. Incidentally, a 427cid-engined Cobra-based special ran in the same race and was, though definitely not an 'official' prototype, an interesting portent of the future.

Three Cobra coupés were entered for Le Mans on June 20/21, 1964. Two were Daytonas for Gurney/Bondurant and Amon/Neerpasch, the third was a coupé built and entered by AC. Incidentally, AC had done much of their testing of this car on public roads, at highly illegal speeds; a fact not unnoticed by the British Press – or Brockbank the famous cartoonist. The resulting publicity led to much speculation about the new 'road' car AC were developing! The AC car, to be driven by Sears/Bolton, had the same overall shape as the Daytona but was easily identifiable by the prominent 'eyebrows' over the wheel arches

and a generally more aggressive appearance.

A quarter of the way through the race, the AC coupé crashed and was unable to continue. Then two-thirds of the way through the race the Amon/Neerpasch Daytona was disqualified following a routine pit stop during which the coupé's engine was restarted with jump leads. This left Gurney/Bondurant to defend Cobra honours, which they did, despite oil cooler problems, crossing the finish line fourth overall – significantly, ahead of the GTOs and behind three Ferrari prototypes – and first in class.

As a background to this glamorous international racing, Cobras in many forms were still doing very well in American domestic racing – a very important role for the Cobra as far as Ford was concerned. After all, their association with the Cobra generated valuable publicity, justifying their backing of the Shelby organisation. However, there was a cloud on the horizon as far as domestic motorsport and the Cobra were concerned – Chevrolet were developing a 7-litre Corvette!

'There is no substitute for cubic inches ...' The 427

Thus, during the latter half of 1964 the Shelby/AC/Ford team were busy developing a 7-litre Cobra to combat the GM threat. Ford were helpful in two respects. First, they were prepared to make available their relatively light and very powerful 427cid V8 – an engine which in NASCAR (stock car racing) form generated 425bhp. Also, because of the Cobra's importance to their corporate image they were prepared to provide computer assistance and suspension experts in order to develop the Cobra's chassis sufficiently to handle the additional power of the 427.

AC started building the first 427 chassis in October 1964. The revised chassis featured stronger main tubes set further apart and with better bracing. AC were also able to put a practical interpretation on the stream of suspension ideas which crossed the Atlantic from Ford.

The new generation chassis sported coil-spring suspension; this not only gave more suspension travel and full independence to each wheel but was also fully adjustable and rose-jointed. Careful planning of geometry gave the set-up built-in anti-dive and anti-squat characteristics.

Bodywise, AC's answer to clothing the wider chassis was to widen a 289 body by the appropriate amount and to give it flared wheel arches to cover the wider wheels/tyres with which the 427 would be fitted. The 427 prototype also sported a larger grille opening in anticipation of the cooling requirements of the larger engine.

Apparently an engine for this first pilot car was shipped in from the USA, allowing initial shakedown testing to take place at Silverstone. A second pilot car was completed at Thames Ditton before the end of 1964, and then full scale production started as Shelby had ordered one hundred 427s in competition trim, in an attempt to homologate the new model for the 1965 season – AC being expected to build at least two cars a day. Production of the 427 marked the end of the line for the original leaf-spring 289 Cobra, of which in total 580 examples had been built.

As a matter of interest, amongst these last 289s was a batch of thirty cars with Lincoln Cruiseomatic automatic transmission. Four of the 427s would also be built with automatic transmission.

1964 drew to a close with the Cobra again winning the American domestic USRRC championship, a series contested very successfully by the so-called 'USRRC-Roadsters'. These cars were based upon the specification of the FIA-Roadsters previously described, but with subtle modifications to meet the rules of the American series. The USRRC-Roadsters had leaf spring suspension and 289cid engines.

On the FIA world series front, a year's competition in the GT category had drawn to a very frustrating conclusion – Ferrari 84.6 points, Shelby Cobra 78.3 points. Understandably Shelby was angered by this result as the key race – the *Coppa de Europa,* Monza – in which his cars could have clinched the championship, was cancelled due to political arguments engineered by Ferrari. This is probably when Shelby made his well-known promise 'to blow Ferrari's ass off' in 1965.

For Shelby American, 1965 started with the first public showing of the new 427 Cobra roadster at Riverside International Raceway, California. Simultaneously, the Shelby Mustang GT350 made its debut – the series of special Mustangs which would result from this first car are very important in terms of automotive history, but are not part of the Cobra story.

The production 427 was a vastly refined car in relation to the 289 which it replaced – despite the fact that all initial 427s were basically pure competition cars. The car was tractable around town – so long as you did not open the progressive carburettors beyond their first stage, after which your eyeballs were pressed back into their sockets as the car headed for the horizon as if launched by a steam catapult! Simply, the 427 did just about everything better than the 289 – and that was quite an achievement.

Apart from the body and chassis modifications incorporated into the original two pilot cars, the production cars featured vertical cut-outs just inboard of the headlights – these were for cockpit cooling on road cars, brake cooling on racing cars. The 427s flanks had a less pronounced tumblehome towards the sills, allowing greater interior space at floor level; the fuel filler was relocated to the right-hand rear wing; 7.5J Halibrand wheels with three-eared knock-off spinners made their debut; and the exhaust system now exited at the rear of the car.

The 427's interior, which, initially at least, always came in black, was little changed from the 289. The seats were slightly larger, there was more interior space widthways, and the instrument panel had been rationalised.

As previously stated, these original 427s came with what was effectively a full-house competition Ford 427cid engine, complete with two massive Holley four-barrel carburettors. Not only was this engine expensive to buy, but it was also in short supply. As a result many 427s were actually fitted with a 428cid V8 intended for the Police Interceptor version of the Ford Galaxie. This unit pumped out 355bhp in Shelby trim, and it was said that the power loss was hardly noticeable on the road; this engine was certainly less 'nervous' and more tractable.

To sum up, the 427 certainly delivered the 'Total Performance' promised in Ford's contemporary ads.

Fairly early in 1965, after just over 50 competition 427s had been delivered to California, it became obvious that it would be impossible to build sufficient cars to allow homologation for the 1965 season. Shelby American had production switched from competition cars to street cars. This left Carroll Shelby with a problem: he had over 50 competition Cobras, and yet did not have a big enough market for the unhomologated cars to be absorbed by racing privateers.

The solution was the Cobra 427S/C – the ultimate road-going Cobra (perhaps the ultimate road-going car?). 'S/C' stood for 'Semi/Competition'. Basically, what Shelby had done was to take a competition car and give it the minimum requirements for legal road use. Problem solved! Each S/C still retained the majority of the competition car's features, right down to the roll bar – which, incidentally, always had a rearward facing brace on the 427 instead of the 289's forward facing item. (The pilot 427s had 289-type roll bars).

Around mid-1965 a semi-mythical beast called a 'Slalomsnake' was announced. This was an off-the-shelf racer, all ready for autocross, slalom or driving test events. If the model ever really existed, it was probably an attempt to use up the last of those 427 competition cars.

AC 289 & AC 428

Back in England, AC were not only building chassis/body units for the 427 but were also busy dropping 289cid Ford V8s into 427 chassis and selling them in Europe and the UK as the 'AC 289' (Mk III). AC had also despatched one of the 427 chassis, complete with 427-type engine, to Frua in Italy. They wanted a more sophisticated Grand Tourer for Europe and Frua obliged with an elegant coupé/drophead design which became the 'AC 428'. This new car made its public debut at Earls Court, London, in October 1965. It was standing alongside a white 7-litre Cobra in full race trim.

In motorsport, 1965 was the heyday of the Cobra. In the international field, the combat-hardened 289cid Daytonas fulfilled Shelby's promise and 'beat the ass off the Ferraris' – bringing the World Manufacturers' Championship for GT Cars to an American manufacturer for the first time in history! At home Cobras swept the board in the SCCA's A/Production class – a feat they would repeat in 1966, 1967, 1968 and 1973.

On this high note the Cobra was withdrawn from FIA competition to make way for Ford's two-seasons-old baby, the Ford GT40 which was showing enormous potential. For the same reason a 427-engined Daytona 'Super Coupé' on which Pete Brock had been working was aborted – imagine the embarrassment if it had beaten the ST40s.

March 1966 saw the introduction of a new Cobra 'Dragonsnake'. Like the earlier version this was a purpose-built drag racer, this time fitted with the 427-type engine.

By 1967 the writing was on the wall for the Cobra in its main market, America. Impending Federal legislation on emissions and crashability, higher fuel and insurance costs, and a generally more puritanical attitude to high-performance cars all conspired to kill the Cobra's appeal. Against this backdrop, Cobra production ended in Venice – although in his book *Shelby American Guide,* Richard J. Kopec said that there were still two unsold 427 Cobras, in San Francisco, as late as 1968. I wonder if they are still there ...? Altogether 356 427-type Cobras were built.

Towards the end of 427 production, Shelby built two very special Cobras – one for himself, and one for comedian Bill Cosby. Based on Cobra 427s, each of these cars featured a supercharged, 700bhp engine and automatic transmission. The 0-60 time was a claimed 3.8 seconds! The Cosby car, CSX3303, was crashed by a subsequent owner and the chassis remains acquired by British specialist Brian Angliss. Partway

through the restoration in England the car was bought by Rod Leach who had it finished as a standard 427 with right-hand drive and manual transmission. Subsequently this car was sold but its British registration 'COB 1' was retained for the twin-turbo Cobra that Rod was having built.

During 1967, Shelby Automotive moved to Ionia, Michigan, to concentrate on the Shelby Mustangs and the company's many other, by now, diverse interests. In 1968, the 'Cobra' name which was now the property of FoMoCo was appended to two Mustangs, the Shelby Cobra GT350 and GT500.

During 1969 production of the AC 289 ended after 27 cars had been built. The AC 428 stayed in production until as late as 1973.

The AC Mk IV and C.P. Autokraft

For many years Brian Angliss has been a Cobra specialist, his Cobra Parts company originally offering restoration services as well as the supply of replacement Cobra parts. Demand from thoughout the world for chassis and body components became so strong that Brian Angliss was able to acquire the original jigs and body formers for the Cobra from AC. These allowed the production of complete new chassis/body units.

A new company, C.P. Autokraft, was formed to build complete new 'Cobras' of which the first batch of 50 are under construction as this is written. These new cars, which feature a very much improved coil-spring type chassis as well as a slightly larger cockpit, are so good that AC have granted C.P.A. a 25-year licence to use the 'AC' badge on their cars and Ford have agreed to sell the car through their dealer network in the USA. In the latter case the intention is that rolling chassis/body units will be shipped to Jack Roush Performance Engineering in Livonia, Michigan, for the installation of Ford's current high performance 302cid V8 of 220bhp (DIN – not the inflated American horses once associated with the Cobra). With the available off-the-shelf tuning components the output of this engine can be taken to over 400bhp – nearly as much as the 427/428, but from a lighter unit.

The quality of the C.P. Autokraft car, officially called 'AC Mk4', is superb and the finished article is almost indistinguishable from a 427-type Cobra – even the alloy wheels are exact replicas of the original Halibrands. Initially, these cars will be expensive; however, after the first fifty units the company hopes to productionize manufacture and therefore bring the price down.

Incidentally, one of the world's best-known Cobras, Rod Leach's 7-litre, twin-turbo, COB 1, is an Autokraft car, but based on an original AC chassis.

SPECIFICATION

Specification*

Type	AC 'Cobra'/Shelby Cobra/Ford Cobra
Built	Thames Ditton, England and Sante Fe, California (approx first thirty cars) then Venice, California.
Engine	Ford cast iron V8. *260cid (4260cc)*, 96.5 x 73mm, 260 bhp at 5800rpm, 269lb ft torque at 4800 rpm. *289cid (4727cc):* 101.6 x 72.8mm, 271bhp at 5800rpm, 269lb ft torque at 4800. *427cid (6998cc):* 107.6 x 96mm, 425bhp at 6000rpm, 480lb ft torque at 3700rpm. *428cid (7013cc):* 104.9 x 101mm, 355bhp at 5200rpm, 390lb ft torque at 3700rpm.
Transmission	Ford. *260:* first 2.36/1, second 1.78/1, third 1.41/1, fourth 1/1, final drive 3.54/1. *289:* first 2.36/1, second 1.61/1, third 1.2/1, fourth 1/1, final drive 4.56/1. 427/428: first 2.32/1, second 1.69/1, third 1/29/1, fourth 1/1, final drive 3.54/1 (427) or 3.31/1 (428). Single plate dry clutch, all models – 10.5in (289)/11.5in (427 & 428). Approximately 30 289 Cobras were built with automatic transmission.
Wheelbase	All models 90 inches
Track (front)	53.25in (260 & 289)/56in (427 & 428)
Track (rear)	52.5in (260 & 289)/56in (427 & 428)
Length	151.5 in (260 & 289)/156in (427 & 428)
Width	61in (260 & 289)/68in (427 & 428)
Height	To top of screen: 45in (260 & 289)/49in (427 & 428)
Weight	2020lb (260), 2100lb (289), 2150lb (427), 2529lb (428)

Suspension	*260 & 289:* Independent, by two transverse leaf springs fixed on central chassis turrets. Leaf springs form upper link to king pins, lower link by A-arm. Telescopic dampers. *427 & 428:* Independent, by coil springs, coaxial dampers and double wishbones. Trailing arms to locate rear wishbones
Steering	Worm and sector (first 100 to 120 cars), then rack and pinion. 3 turns lock-to-lock for rack and pinion. $1\frac{2}{3}$ worm and sector
Rear axle	Centrally mounted Salisbury hypoid differential unit, with PowrLok limited slip. Open halfshaft to rear hubs, each with two universal joints and a sliding spline
Brakes	Hydraulic. Four wheel discs. Most common size $11\frac{5}{8}$in front, $10\frac{3}{4}$in rear
Chassis	Two large diameter steel tubes jointed ladder-fashion form backbone. Turrets fore and aft carry suspension and differential unit. Cage of smaller diameter steel tubes strengthen main chassis and support bodywork and bulkheads. Substantial detail improvement and strengthening of chassis, including larger diameter main tubes, for coil spring models, although basic structure unchanged
Body	Hand-formed 18 gauge alloy sheets, supported by lattice of small diameter steel tubes
Wheels & tyres	Wire wheels 6J x 15 on knock-off hubs, tyres 6.50/6.70 x 15 (260) 7.35 x 15 crossply or 185 x 15 radial (289). Halibrand alloy 7.5J x 15 on knock-off peg-drive hubs, tyres 8.15 x 15 crossply or 205 x 15 radials (427 & 428)
Electrical system	Dynamo (most 289s), alternator (427/428). 12 volt. Ignition by coil and distributor
Performance	*260:* 136mph, 0-60 5.2 secs, quarter mile 13.8 secs, 18mpg (Imp). *289:* 138mph, 0-60 5.5 secs, quarter mile 13.9 secs, 17mpg (Imp.) *427:* 145mph, 0-60 4.2 secs, quarter mile 12.4 secs, 12mpg (Imp). *428:* 140mph, 0.60 5.9secs, quarter mile 14.9 secs, 12mpg

*Note. In theory these specifications represent 'standard' road cars. However it must be understood that an enormous amount of optional equipment was always available for both road and competition cars – this equipment could be specified on new cars or added after purchase. It is also true that when improved components became available as part of the Cobra's natural evolution, they were often retro-fitted to older cars – the 289cid engine is a good case in point. Another important point is that the 'AC 289', 95 built from 1966, was in fact based on the 427-type chassis – therefore some of the specifications given under the '427' category will apply to the AC 289.

MOTOR   week ending November 25 1967

ROAD TESTS

7-litre adrenalin pump

Driving the world's fastest road dragster   **by Roger Bell**

NO doubt Mrs. Castle would consider 500 horsepower a fair ration for 10 cars but somehow Messrs. Ford, Shelby, and Holman and Moody have managed to pack them all into one. As an insurance risk, it doesn't rate very highly, either; the premiums on a submarine with a canvas hood would probably be lower. Despite the bureaucratic gloom, though, we not only lived but actually enjoyed a bit of perverted motoring in the world's fastest accelerating production car. Fastest? Look at the figures. If there is any other road car around that can beat this AC Shelby Cobra 427 to 100 m.p.h. then we'd like to drive it. All offers will be acknowledged in writing. . . .

The car has an interesting history. Ed Feutel, a wealthy American lawyer, bought a pair of 427s from Shelby, one fully modified for racing and the other for use as a road car in a milder state of tune. Midway through "doing" the European circuits with Tony Settember as co-driver, Feutel decided his road car wasn't quick enough and ordered a go-faster Shelby conversion for the engine. Virtually the only difference between the two now is the exhaust (open side drain-pipes on the racer, semi-civilized on the road car), the brakes (GT40-based on the racer) and the camshafts. In the interests of tractability, the shopping car has a "quieter" cam profile than the other, which is reputed to develop 550 gross b.h.p. Since no one seems to know, we can only guess that the soft-cam version of this 427 (not to be confused with the entirely different cooking 428 which has hydraulic lifters and considerably less strength) has over 500 b.h.p. in round numbers. At any rate, the power is adequate.

When the two cars were eventually put up for sale John Woolfe beat Prince Rainier on the cheque-book draw, brought his brace of Cobras to England and, despite assurances that it couldn't be done, had the road car converted to right-hand drive. As the Club dicers know, the racer he raced with considerable success, collecting 10 firsts, and five seconds in 16 starts, before selling out to hill-climb driver John Macklin. The other one he lent to us for a few days, noble fellow. Just to prove that we are utterly corruptible when it comes to cars as fast as this, our thanks to him are tendered as a free, editorial advertisement; the car is for sale, price £3,750. For further details, read on.

It is the wheels and tyres that give it away as being something extraordinary. Three-eared nuts secure the magnificent magnesium Halibrand wheels shod with ultra-low-profile Firestone Grand Prix tyres made of a compromise wet-or-dry rubber mix. Each of the monster 12.00 x 15 back covers plants around 80 sq. inches of rubber on the road, the 9.20 x 15 fronts slightly less. The spare (which fills the boot) was another compromise—10.30 x 15 so that it can be used reasonably on the front or back wheels. The behaviour of these massive racing tyres serves as a classic example of why they are generally unsuitable for road use, despite their uncanny cornering and braking powers. To start with, the covers are wafer thin so they puncture quite easily—as Jim Clark has found in several formula races this year. Ours had tubes in them for additional protection though in fact we escaped any blow outs. In the thin-wall construction lies the secret of their remarkable weight: picking the spare out of the boot was like

lifting an alloy kettle you thought was full of water but wasn't. Worn on featherweight wheels of an identical pattern to those used on some Indianapolis cars, they are incredibly light for the size. On smooth dry roads the adhesion seems to be limitless but on any other sort of surface you begin to realize that there are many other facets of road tyre performance which are all too easily taken for granted. Driving over mediocre secondary roads feels like riding a Victorian train on crooked rails. Every little ridge, white line, Cats-Eye stud and bump deflect the car sideways—though the action is self-correcting, west-bound deflections cancelling out those going east by the law of averages. This curious behaviour is typical of any square-edged racing tyre but is almost certainly exaggerated, we discovered later, by some play in the wishbone linkages (since re-bushed) on the Cobra. It is virtually impossible to provoke tyre squeal—except by spinning the wheels on take-off—but the tremendous thrummmm on a coarse surface made granite chippings sound like Belgian pavé. Even in heavy rain, ordinary tyres will cut through the puddles on a water-logged road but wide un-siped racing covers are not at their best when afloat. Delivering 500 to a dry surface is exciting enough but power boating we prefer to leave to masochistic seamen. Little wonder that the red stop lights went on at Indianapolis this year when it rained!

There is, however, a clear distinction between the performance on drenched roads to that on merely a damp or wet surface. You still have to treat the throttle like of piece of Dresden china but even when reigning back a couple of hundred horses, the tyres can cope

Performance

	Cobra 427	AC 289	Jaguar E 4.2
Max speed	165	134.9	150.0
	m.p.h.	m.p.h.	m.p.h.
Acceleration	(see text)		
	sec.	sec.	sec.
0—30 m.p.h.	1.8	2.5	2.7
0—40	2.6	3.4	3.7
0—50	3.4	4.4	4.8
0—60	4.2	5.6	7.0
0—70	5.7	7.2	8.6
0—80	6.8	9.0	11.0
0—90	8.5	11.3	13.9
0—100	10.3	13.7	17.2
0—110	13.1	17.9	21.0
0—120	16.4	22.8	25.2
standing ¼-mile	12.4	14.4	14.9
top gear	sec.	sec.	sec.
20—40 m.p.h.	3.2	3.9	5.5
30—50	3.4	4.2	5.4
40—60	3.6	4.2	5.3
50—70	3.9	4.3	6.0
60—80	4.1	4.4	6.6
70—90	4.1	4.7	6.6

80—100	4.1	5.0	7.3
90—110	4.7	6.1	7.3
100—120	6.5	8.0	7.8
in third	sec.	sec.	sec.
20—40 m.p.h.	2.7	3.6	4.4
30—50	2.6	3.6	4.2
40—60	2.7	3.4	4.0
50—70	2.8	3.5	4.4
60—80	2.8	3.8	4.7
70—90	2.9	3.9	4.8
80—100	3.3	4.7	5.9
90—110	4.3	—	6.9
Consumption at	m.p.g.	m.p.g.	m.p.g.
30 m.p.h.	17.4	27.4	27.8
40	17.1	25.6	29.4
50	17.1	23.5	28.2
60	16.0	21.6	27.6
70	14.8	19.4	26.2
80	13.8	17.5	24.0
90	13.2	16.2	22.5
100	12.1	14.8	20.2
overall	see text	15.2	18.5
touring	see text	16.3	21.5

well enough with what's left. So even though this must be the world's easiest car to spin round the gearlever on a wet road it remains a potent performer even in imperfect conditions. Unlike the 4.7-litre 289 we tested recently, which could be hurled round corners almost tail first on opposite lock, the 7-litre liked to travel with the back wheels squarely behind the fronts. These racing tyres are

either rolling or going sideways and the difference between the two is about 0.001 degrees. It is easy enough to tighten your cornering line by adjusting slip angles with the throttle but hanging the tail out demands such instant reflexes and delicacy that it is unwise even to try it except when the coast is very

Continued on the next page

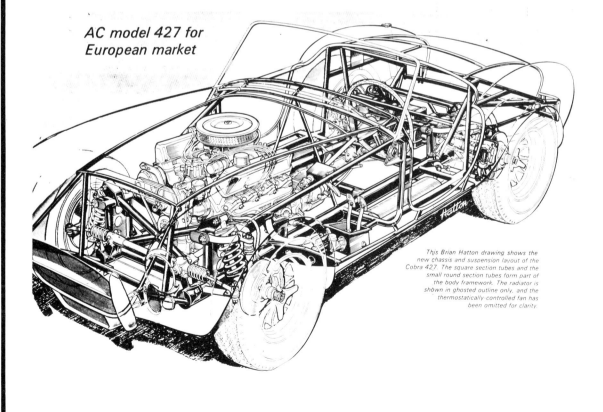

AC model 427 for European market

This Brian Hatton drawing shows the new chassis and suspension layout of the Cobra 427. The square section tubes and the small round section tubes form part of the body framework. The radiator is shown in ghosted outline only, and the thermostatically-controlled fan has been omitted for clarity.

7-litre adrenalin pump

continued

clear. Stubbornly attempting to master this pointless technique did at least achieve one unexpected bonus: like the Formula 3 driver who went karting to hone his reaction times, so opposite lockery on any other car seemed contemptuously easy after practice in the 427. Curiously, we didn't need to exercise any caution with the brakes, which could be slammed on in the wet without locking the wheels. In fact you *need* to slam them on because with hard fade-free linings and no servo, they are very, very heavy.

Fortunately it remained dry for performance testing at MIRA, the only place we could really let the car go. Join us on the acceleration strip. A peaceful scene. The car burbles lazily like a brace of paraffin tractors pausing at the end of the furrow. You blip the throttle and the whole thing quivers as the gigantic torque tries to flip the chassis round the crankshaft just to show there is nothing agricultural about this machine. About 3,000 r.p.m. and a heavy boot is enough.

Suddenly you've been rammed hard from behind. Your passenger disappears backwards, your head feels like a lump of lead on a straw neck and pungent rubber smoke pours into the cockpit by some strange trick of aerodynamics. Until the car's speed catches up with the spinning back wheels the tail weaves from side to side and the air is filled with wild screeching noises (as well as smoke), quickly super-

Even with about 160 sq. in. of racing rubber on road, the enormous power can easily provoke smoky wheel spin.

seded by a hysterical howl as the massive V-8 gets up on the cam and surges on to 7,000 r.p.m. You grab second as fast as the heavy long-travel clutch will allow. The car bucks and wriggles as the concrete ridges deflect the unforgiving tyres but the steering kicks itself straight. The Cape Kennedy g forces continue through second into third by which time you're approaching orbital speed, just to add to the excitement.

The driver isn't the only chap working hard. The observer, trying not to think about the enormous wrench on a makeshift fifth wheel bracket, is breaking all records, too, clicking stop-watches as though he is playing the piano. The available timepieces ran out after 22.5 seconds (the standing kilometer time) having, on the best run, recorded 40 m.p.h.

MOTOR week ending November 25 1967

in 2.6 seconds, 60 m.p.h. in 4.2, 80 m.p.h. in 6.4, 100 m.p.h. in 9.8 and the quarter mile post in a prodigious 12.4 seconds. All right, so some dragsters can do it quicker but is there another road car in the world to beat these figures? I doubt it.

The distressing thing is that we are now deprived of looking forward to anything better in the foreseeable future. At least, not on acceleration. There are perhaps one or two other cars around with higher maximum speeds; this particular Cobra was geared for 165 m.p.h. at 7,000 r.p.m. though with a higher final drive ratio, it could perhaps do better than this. Even on MIRA's relatively short straights, it reached over 150 m.p.h.; coming off the banking at around 125 m.p.h. (as fast as seemed prudent since the tyres kept clambering up the ridges towards the retainer barrier) the car gained another 25-odd m.p.h. 600 yds farther on before breaking the electronic trap at a best of 148.8 m.p.h. A further gain of 200 r.p.m. before breaking hard for the banking—an odd experience—took the speed up to around 153 m.p.h. which is probably the highest that MOTOR has attained in road testing, and certainly the highest we have reached at MIRA.

One of the many remarkable things about this 427 was that it could play a docile Jekyll just as well as a ferocious Hyde. On the road, it was little short of showmanship to use anything other than top gear which could drag the car from 30 to 100 m.p.h. in 13.5 seconds (quicker than an E-type can do it through the gears) and waffle smoothly at 20 m.p.h. in traffic. The heavyish long-travel clutch does not exactly encourage frequent gear-work in town, anyway—though considering it must be built to battleship proportions to absorb so much torque, the gearbox is really magnificent. The big chrome lever, spring-loaded into the 3-4 plane, has a crisp well-oiled movement, marred only by a little notchiness when you tax the unbeatable synchromesh by trying to snatch the gears at high r.p.m. As on most big American V-8s, the splendid throttle linkage has a long progressive travel which allows the smooth, delicate control you need with so much power on tap. Fuel consumption is, well, heavy. There was no mileage recorder on the car so we can't quote an overall figure. But comparing the specifics in the data with those of the 289 suggests a thirst of between 11 and 15 m.p.g. depending not so much on how fast you drive as on how frequently and hard you employ the lower ratios for acceleration.

The enormous tyres and bulging wings and bonnet, somehow suggestive of an irresistible force about to break loose, seemed to induce tremendous awe and respect among our road fellows who would invariably gawk in their mirrors and pull over, acknowledging by instinct that they were not quite in the same league. (One fellow asked incredulously at the lights: "What's that then, a Panhard . . .?"). Such courtesy we acclaim even though it was seldom necessary since the Cobra needs little outside assistance for overtaking. A brief blast in second and you're past, braking for the next car while the fellow behind is still looking in the mirror wondering where you went. The novelty of such violent stop-go driving would no doubt wear thin after a while; even during our brief few days with the car, 30 m.p.h. signs began to offer a welcome respite.

In other respects, the 427 was very similar to the 289. Leaky, draughty and generally pretty uncivilized in creature comforts by today's grand touring standards. But then who wants to buy an adrenalin pump to relax?

M

Over 500 horsepower will rocket this heavy car over a quarter mile from rest in 12.4 sec.

Worm's eye view of the 9.50 x 15 Firestone racing tyres: those on the back are even bigger.

The cockpit (bottom left) has nothing more than the bare essentials, and creature comforts are minimal.

Only the 427 Cobra labels on the chrome rocker covers identify the great chunk of engine as something special (below right).

The A.C. Cobra

POWERED BY *Ford*

THE A.C. Cobra is at present an export-only model. It is based very closely on the A.C. Ace, which normally carries a Bristol or Ford Zephyr engine. Suitably strengthened to withstand an American Ford V8 unit of 4¾ litres capacity, the Cobra is manufactured at the A.C. factory at Thames Ditton and shipped to the States, where car and engine meet. About 10 Cobras per week are sent over to Shelby American, Inc., who are selling them like hot cakes.

The A.C. chassis was designed by John Tojeiro, and was in fact based on the very successful Bristol-engined "Toj" raced by Cliff Davis. It has a ladder-type tubular frame, with independent suspension at both ends by transverse springs and wishbones. The Cobra has tubes of heavier gauge and the shorter Vee-type engine has permitted the insertion of extra cross-bracing. Rack and pinion steering and anti-roll torsion bars front and rear are additions to the specification, and naturally the differential and universally jointed half-shafts are heavier. The differential is of the self-locking variety and the track has been slightly increased, both front and rear.

Panelled in aluminium, the open two-seater body has a lower grille and bonnet than that which the overall height of the Bristol engine demands. The Ford unit, with its own all-synchromesh four-speed gearbox, is in fact notably compact. With the over-square dimensions of 101.6 mm. x 72.9 mm. (4,727 c.c.), it probably develops around 275 b.h.p. in touring trim and over 350 b.h.p. when tuned for racing. All this in a car weighing some 18 cwt. can only result in a simply shattering performance.

I was thus more than delighted when, during some glass-lifting exercises at the Steering Wheel, Carroll Shelby suggested that I should borrow his personal Cobra for a day To make the most of the occasion, that day started before 5 a.m.! Carroll had remarked that the car was "set up for the street", which means that it was neither geared for an ultimate maximum speed nor fitted with the greatest available number of carburetters It was, in fact, far more flexible

on top gear than any luxury limousine and its traffic manners were impeccable.

What can one do with a car which will out-accelerate practically anything on the road when top gear is engaged at 15 m.p.h., yet has about the best close-ratio gearbox that could be imagined? The desire to feel that "whoosh" of power from zero revs. on top is always competing with the excitement of rushing past 50 m.p.h. on bottom gear. With the final drive ratio fitted to the test car, 6,500 r.p.m. came up at once in top and I lifted my foot. This resulted in a timed speed of 136 m.p.h., but of course 150 m.p.h. could be exceeded with a suitable crown wheel and pinion in place.

The engine must be praised very highly indeed. A new lightweight Ford model, it is utterly smooth at all speeds up to 6,500 r.p.m., and would certainly go much higher if one turned a blind

eye to the dial. The clutch copes happily with the mammoth torque and the four synchronized gears may be selected with the greatest ease and rapidity. The roads were damp, though not wet, when I started my performance tests, and rain was actually falling at their completion. As a result, the figures which I recorded could be beaten on a dry road. Nevertheless, to accelerate from a standstill to 50 m.p.h. in 3.8 seconds or to 80 m.p.h. in 8.2 seconds is a somewhat dramatic performance.

Very quiet mechanically, the power unit has just a trace of exhaust "beat". This noise, so typical of big V8s, is rather objectionable to most hearers and could probably be eliminated by some cross connection of the two separate exhaust branches. It would appear that V8 noises are accepted in America, but in England they are no more popular than were the single-cylinder detonations

of the 500 c.c. racers. This is a minor point, however.

The A.C. chassis has been improved by the adoption of rack and pinion steering, which is both sensitive and precise in action. The angle of roll during fast cornering has also been greatly reduced by the front and rear torsion bars. At fast touring speeds, the Cobra is easy to handle and the sheer luxury of having all that power in reserve is one of motoring's greatest sensual pleasures.

Driven to the limit, the Cobra is not for the beginner. To start with, it is a foot shorter in the wheelbase than other cars of comparable potency, such as the Ferrari, so one tends to be rather busy when drifting fast curves on full throttle. I admit that my test was too short to allow me to get to know the car, and I am sure that I would have gained confi-

dence with experience. The machine is being improved with the rapidity which results from racing a new model, and I expect that it will become easier to handle in spite of its spectacular performance. In any case, it is only when driven at racing speeds that the Cobra demands considerable skill.

The traction afforded by the independent rear suspension, plus the self-locking differential, renders extremely rapid starts particularly easy to carry out. The disc brakes on all four wheels are immune from fading, but demand quite a lot of pedal pressure for emergency stops at fairly low speeds. Continuous use of the brakes from high speeds causes them no distress whatsoever, which is a comfort when so much performance is available.

Well-made and attractively finished, the aluminium body is of that excellence

for which A.C.s are renowned. The hood does not flap, though it naturally bulges a little at over 120 m.p.h. American instruments were fitted to the test car with proper round faces, but the speedometer was inoperative so I calibrated the rev. counter, which was notably steady. I found the seating position very comfortable and the ride was good over all but the worst bumps.

The A.C. Cobra is a high-quality sports car with a stupendous performance. It is outstandingly flexible and has perfect town manners, while it may be driven everywhere on top gear or run at high speeds on the close indirect ratios, according to the whim of the moment. It is by no means heavy on petrol and its great reserve of power, when sensibly used, must be regarded as an excellent safety feature on crowded roads.

SPECIFICATION AND PERFORMANCE DATA

Car Tested: A.C. Cobra sports two-seater, price (America only) $5,995.

Engine: Eight cylinders 101.6 mm. x 72.9 mm. (4,727 c.c.). Pushrod-operated overhead valves. Compression ratio 9.2 to 1. 275 b.h.p. at 5,800 r.p.m. Four-choke downdraught carburetter. Two Ford ignition coils and Spalding distributor.

Transmission: Long single dry plate clutch. Borg-Warner four-speed all-synchromesh gearbox with short central lever, ratios 3.77, 5.29, 6.71 and 8.89 to 1. Hypoid final drive with self-locking differential.

Chassis: Ladder-type tubular frame. Independent front and rear suspension by transverse leaf springs and wishbones, with telescopic dampers and anti-roll torsion bars front and rear. Rack and pinion steering. Knock-on wire wheels fitted

6.50/6.70 x 15 ins. tyres. Disc brakes all round.

Equipment: 12-volt lighting and starting. Speedometer, rev.-counter, oil and water thermometers, oil pressure and fuel gauges, ammeter, clock. Flashing direction indicators. Heating and demisting. Windscreen wipers and washers.

Dimensions: Wheelbase 7 ft. 6 ins. Track (front) 4 ft. 3¼ ins., (rear) 4 ft. 4¼ ins. Overall length 12 ft. 7⅛ ins. Width 5 ft. 1 in. Turning circle 34 ft. Weight 18 cwt.

Performance: Maximum speed 136 m.p.h. Speeds in gears: 3rd 96 m.p.h., 2nd 75 m.p.h., 1st 56 m.p.h. Standing quarter-mile (damp road) 13.8 secs. Acceleration: 0-30 m.p.h. 2.5 secs., 0-50 m.p.h. 3.8 secs., 0-60 m.p.h. 5.2 secs., 0-80 m.p.h. 8.2 secs., 0-100 m.p.h. 13 secs.

Fuel Consumption: 14 to 18 m.p.g. (approx.).

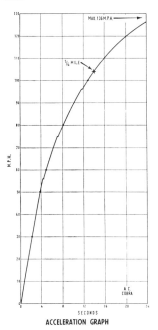

ACCELERATION GRAPH

OWNER'S VIEW

The author interviews Cobra-owner John Haynes, a lifelong car enthusiast, and founder/chairman of the Haynes Publishing Group. John has a large collection of high-performance cars and is therefore able to judge the Cobra on its true merits in relation to the other cars which might be considered its peers.

RTG. When and why, did you buy your Cobra?

JHH. I bought it about eight years ago. I'd always wanted one, and it seemed to me to be the ultimate what I call 'traditional' sports car: that is, an open two-seater. I'd seen them racing and they were obviously so enormously powerful that I thought, that's got to be the most incredible car to drive. I also think the Cobra looks gorgeous; it's got the most beautiful shape – it's just a very desirable motor car and I'm jolly glad I did buy mine eight years ago!

RTG. When you'd actually bought one and you got it home, was it what you expected?

JHH. When I brought it home it was very disappointing because, unknown to me, the tyre pressures were all wrong, and it was raining! It was tremendously noisy with the hood up, and every time I accelerated the car lurched from one side of the road to the other

because of those incorrect tyre pressures. It wasn't until I got it home and was able to sort that out, and we had a sunny day, that I was really able to take it out and absolutely revel in the Cobra's performance.

RTG. And do you use it quite often now?

JHH. Not really, although I'd like to use it more. I use it at weekends and occasionally during the week if it's really fine. It's the sort of car that's tremendous to drive for about forty miles maximum and then you want to get into something civilised!

RTG. Why? Is it because of the noise?

JHH. It's a hard ride especially with thinly upholstered bucket seats: it's a real sports car! It *is* noisy, and it's just very draining to drive. Tremendous fun, but at the same time, if you want to go any distance ... I daresay if I were a very young man I might enjoy driving long distances!

RTG. What kind of handling and performance does the car have?

JHH. Utterly exhilarating! As far as I'm concerned it's the most exciting open two-seater sports car that I've ever driven, and I've driven quite a few including things like Corvettes and E-types.

RTG. So, how do you think a 427 Cobra would be?

JHH. I don't think that would be quite as nice. I haven't actually driven one, but have talked to people who have and they say it's a much heavier car up front, and it lacks agility. The 289 Cobra is a much more chuckable car, you can do all sorts of crazy things with it and not get into trouble. I don't know how Lord Cross kept spinning his! You can slide it: in fact, there's so much power that you can power slide it through corners.

RTG. Doesn't it tend to understeer with all that weight up front?

JHH. No, I wouldn't have said so because you've got so much power to put down at the back that you can swing the tail out, and it's very well balanced too, I think it's got

pretty close to 50-50 weight distribution.

RTG. Has your car won any prizes in concours or similar events?

JHH. No, because it's not quite good enough to go into concours.

RTG. Do you enter your Cobra in any form of motorsport?

JHH. No, I must admit I wouldn't like to put it at risk in motorsport. I have done the odd sprint with it, but nothing more than that; I wouldn't take it circuit racing ...

RTG. I suppose, because Cobras have become so valuable, the way you use it must always be tempered by the knowledge of what it's worth?

JHH. Yes, there are a number of people who do race their Cobras and that's fine, that's superb. But it *was* built as a road-going car, and I get enormous enjoyment out of it on the roads; I just don't feel the need to prove it in competition – I know what it is, I know how it goes, I can understand people wanting to race them but as far as I'm concerned I get so much fun out of driving it on ordinary roads, in good weather, that that's enough.

RTG. What sort of condition was the car in when you bought it?

JHH. Good condition. I've found over the years that buying cars in bad condition and trying to get them into good shape is not only very expensive but very time-consuming – I don't have the necessary time so I made sure it was in good condition when I bought it. Anyway, it's got an aluminium body and that had un-retouched original paintwork. It had done in the region of 50,000 miles so that big V8 engine was still in good condition, synchromesh in second was getting a little weak – it's a very, very fast change. It's amazing that a car, which on paper seems so bulky with a big V8 engine, should be so manoeuvrable and chuckable and just be so much, to my mind, the ultimate sports car.

RTG. Is the running cost high; that is, in terms of petrol consumption?

JHH. No, petrol consumption – I

haven't really measured it — I suppose must be somewhere in the region of about 18 mpg, the car's so light you see, if you accelerate really hard you're not using up gallons of fuel to move a two ton body along. Also, the frontal area isn't very great, it's a small car.

RTG. Have you experienced any difficulty in obtaining parts?

JHH. No, none at all. It's a very simple car, very basic as far as the engine and other mechanical components are concerned. The only item that I am having trouble getting hold of is the rev counter drive cable which runs from the back of the dynamo. As Lucas doesn't seem to be able to supply one, I suppose really I ought to advertise for one. In the main it's very straightforward.

RTG. Is there a specialist whom you have found particularly useful?

JHH. Not really as the car has never needed any major work. There is a local engineer who does a lot of work for me, he's worked on my Cord and he's worked on various other of my cars. He completely rebuilt the engine of my Phantom II which, believe it or not, suffered a cracked block in a very bad frost. He's an engineer, he can look at something mechanical and talk about it, and tell you whom he can go to and get parts from and so on.

RTG. Are there any weak areas that you know of that people should look out for?

JHH. Well, as I've said, I'm getting a bit of synchromesh trouble from the gearbox: it's a very fast change, you can move it as fast as your hand can move and I suspect, with all that power and torque coming from the engine, the baulk rings take quite a battering ...

RTG. Is there an owners club or clubs? If so, how helpful is it to be a member? Do they have major meetings?

JHH. There is an AC owners club but I must confess I don't belong to it. It would be interesting to be a member, but then again, I'm president of our local Southern Milestone Motorclub and that has

150 members. We organise all sorts of events all over the country — tours, driving tests, rallies. The club is open to anybody who we consider has an interest in motorcars. It's good because we're not aligned with any one make; I'm not terribly keen on one marque clubs; you get a rivalry sometimes between members as to whose car is better, and so on, and that's a great shame.

RTG. How would you sum up the enjoyment you get from your Cobra?

JHH. Well, it's a combination of acceleration, speed, noise, the wind in your hair. Whenever I've driven it hard, I always get out of the car shaking! I've been out on the road for about 20 minutes in it and I've been really throwing it along — and it can be thrown along — and I know I've been driving it ... The trouble is, after 10 minutes out of the car you want to get back in and do it again!

The thing about a Cobra is the sheer, simple, functional beauty of it. There isn't an ounce of excess weight; take a Cobra door and open it, and it's lightweight aluminium trimmed with just a piece of thin cloth on the inside.

RTG. What advice would you give to potential buyers of a Cobra?

JHH. Some very simple advice; but for owners. Don't sell! The guy I bought mine from would 'phone at regular six-monthly intervals asking to buy it back!

Rod Leach is a Cobra addict who bubbles with enthusiasm as soon as you mention his favourite car. He is a fount of knowledge on the model who, at times, seems to know off by heart the chassis and registration numbers of all the Cobras! Rod runs a company called 'Nostalgia' which specialises in the sale of classic and exotic cars, particularly Cobras, of which more than thirty examples have passed through his hands. Rod also owns COB I, probably the most potent Cobra in captivity with its blueprinted 427 engine and twin turbochargers.

RTG. How did your interest in Cobras begin?

RL. I already had a liking for AC Ace-Bristols: friends of mine had them in the mid-sixties. I saw my first one round about 1963/64, and they were always my favourite of the sporting two-seaters. I then saw in a magazine the first road test of a Cobra that John Bolster did, and the combination of the looks of the AC Ace-Bristol and stunning performance figures just did it for me ... that was it! I saw my first Cobra about a year later, coming back from the West Country, and putting the two things together — the magazine description and actually seeing one in the flesh — ensured that I haven't looked back since. I didn't get one, of course, until August 1973 when after I started up my Company 'Nostalgia', I was determined somehow or other to own one even though, in those days, they were already reaching £3,300 and they had been substantially cheaper than that only a few years earlier.

RTG. How did you come to specialize in Cobras?

RL. I didn't set out to, but I was so enthusiastic about them, and having written in my advertisements that I wanted to acquire and own one, I was then made a totally unikely offer of a brand new Cobra built by AC Cars. I found myself being so excited about it that every advertisement I wrote for *Motor Sport* or *Classic Car* would contain a reference to COB 1, and I suppose my enthusiasm rubbed off on other people. Don't forget the Cobra has always been quite a difficult car to sell and, therefore, somebody specialising, even if not deliberately, probably engendered enthusiasm so that owners of Cobras who were trying to sell their cars would say, "well, you have a go, you seem to like them". The more that happened, the more it seemed to catch on, so much so that I've had on average three Cobras a year for the last eleven or twelve years. Considering there was only a maximum at any one time of 80 Cobras in the UK – I think we're down to about 55 now – that's been quite a fair proportion.

RTG. Did you get to drive every one of them?

RL. Yes, every single one that I've had, I've driven.

RTG. So you must be one of the most experienced Cobra drivers in the world.

RL. No, not really – I've never driven one in motor sport, apart from on 'just for fun' test days. Brian Angliss has probably had more Cobras than I have, I don't know; it would be interesting to ask him if he's ever kept track of all the real, original, Cobras that have gone through his hands, but I don't think he tested every one. I like to give every Cobra that comes through my hands a longish drive, if only to convince myself that the next owner is not going to have problems.

RTG. After wanting a Cobra for so long, when you finally had a Cobra of your own, was it what you expected, or was it an anti-climax?

RL. When I first drove COB 1, there was so much adrenalin going through me that I don't know whether I enjoyed it or not – I was a little frightened as it was a very valuable motor car, and it was quicker than anything else I'd driven. I had been out in a 289 previously, one that was advertised in *Motor Sport,* and I had a quick drive of that and it was quick. I had at the time a Mk. II Sunbeam Tiger and I thought that, with its 4.7-litre engine, was going to be as quick as the Cobra, but the Cobra just disappeared. If the 289 was fast the 7-litre was really something else, but it had done so few miles when I first got it that I was trying to run it in and didn't really open it up for the best part of three or four months, by which time I'd got used to it. I suppose I'm the opposite to Setright – he sees all of the Cobra's faults but none of its virtues, I see all of its virtues and none of its faults! More adjectives have been used to describe Cobras than any

other car that's ever been built, I would think. Most of them extol its virtues and if you take a percentage of those with a pinch of salt, and you're prepared to accept the car for what it is, you will find that it is still the greatest two-seater sports/racing car that's ever been built. It does have its shortcomings, whichever version you get, the 289, the Mk. II, Mk. III or 7-litre. The 7-litre, particularly, can be unforgiving if you're going too quickly into a bend; within limits it's very good and it doesn't have the rotten road-holding people say it does, but I have held my breath on one or two occasions! This is probably something you don't get so much with the 289 – not in the Mk.II. You can use the 289's power most of the time, even on country roads: you can't with the 7-litre, you have to wait for a short straight, give it a burst and then back off.

RTG. What advice would you give to somebody contemplating buying a Cobra?

RL. Buy it now! It's going to be more expensive next year, and get more expensive the year after that ... If you want one, then buy any Cobra that comes up. Even if you're buying a terror, which is unlikely because there are very few Cobras that need restoring, it doesn't matter as the car is eventually going to be worth whatever you put into it. It is one of the very few genuine road-going racing sports cars, which will not just hold their own in terms of value, but will appreciate despite the scepticism from some quarters.

RTG. What about the danger of buying a non-genuine Cobra?

RL. Not really a problem. Every Cobra's got its own individual chassis plate which is documented, not only in this country but in the Cobra world register. In fact, every one is so well documented that you would be hard pushed to end up with a 'funny' one.

RTG. You obviously see Cobras as a solid investment for the future?

RL. Yes, they're keeping ahead of inflation better than any money you

may care to keep in a deposit account. For example, since 1964 the cost of living has gone up by six times. Now in 1964, new Cobras were £2500 and in 1972 they were still about that price. However since 1973 the cost of living's gone up by about three times and now, of course, that £2500 is something like £30,000! That aspect of the Cobra could play a fundamental part in the buying decision.

RTG. How would you sum-up the pleasure you get from a Cobra?

RL. There's nothing else like it, simply nothing else like it. I know that the D-type, of course, is a tremendous road car as well but it wasn't designed to be used on the road – the Cobra was, that's the difference. I don't think there's been any other car built since 1967 that will touch it from zero to a hundred. Nothing, Porsche 3.3 turbo, or even the new GTO Ferrari that's coming out, can beat the Cobra, and that's a standard model Cobra!

The other lovely thing about Cobras is that they are totally docile despite their power, and their looks are timeless ... In fact, an article in *Automobile Quarterly* called them the "Now and Forever Cobra", and that's about right.

RTG. What plans do you have for COB 1? Any more development?

RL. It will be nice to just keep development ticking along. I've gone to the maximum I can get out of the particular turbo-charger system fitted, which makes it quite hairy already! Over the next winter I want to change the rather old fashioned turbo installation for a 'state-of-the-art' system.

RTG. What sort of horsepower do you think you'll be able to dial in with the new system?

RL. Probably, in American figures, about 430 horsepower. A European figure would be 370 horsepower or something like that. I still want to keep the car road-usable and if I thought I might destroy that then I wouldn't modify the car further.

RTG. What do you think the future holds for Cobras?

RL. As a point of concern, I think I might say that the supply of Cobras in the UK is drying up quickly, and partly that's my fault, but I only sell cars that people ask me to sell for them. The fact that overseas markets are so strong in relation to our own means that we will continue to lose cars: we never had that many anyway – 80 maximum, down to about 55 now. In fact, there are only about five or six 7-litre Cobras left in the UK, so therefore the next purge will be on the 289s or the Mk IIs and they too will start disappearing. A lot of similar cars, like the D-type and sports racing Ferraris, have left these shores over the years, leaving just a hard core of cars, which don't come up for sale, but which don't come out to be shown off very often either. The loss of Cobras is my concern. Soon there just won't be enough around, so people won't see them: all they'll have to see are Cobra lookalikes since there won't be any more authentic replicas.

BUYING

Buying

Because of their rarity and the exciting nature of the car, Cobra values have escalated dramatically – so much so, that you are unlikely, to say the least, to find a 'one-owner Cobra in need of attention and going for a song'. The current value of existing examples is so high that they are all well maintained and carefully protected from the elements.

If you are in a position to buy, then careful consideration should be given to selecting the best model for your needs. In the UK choice is very restricted as 260cid and 427/428cid models are as rare as hens' teeth – so you can have any model you like ... so long as it's a 289. You *will* have the choice of leaf or coil spring models and in this respect choice will depend on personal preference: for the better refinement of the coil spring cars or the 'chuckability' of the leaf spring models.

US citizens have the much brighter prospect of having sufficient choice to be in a position to be choosey, as most Cobras ended up on their shores. Here there is no doubt that the 427 (and I mean 427), as the definitive Cobra, is the one to have –

particularly the 427S/C. Second place would probably go to an original and unadulterated 260 – after all, only thirty were built, and they were the *first* Cobras even if they don't offer quite the excitement of the later cars. Of course the rarest of all would be one of the two supercharged 427s which Shelby built or a mythical Slalomsnake. Then there were the competition specials which were built in small numbers: the Daytona coupés, the Le Mans cars and the Le Mans Replicas, the FIA Roadsters and, of course the USRRC Roadsters.

All of this is not to denigrate the road-going 289s and 428s – cars which any enthusiast would be proud to own and are probably the most practical proposition.

Having found your Cobra, a structural check will be worthwhile. Corrosion of a serious nature in the main chassis tubes is rare – although stories have been heard of rusted main chassis tubes being 'repaired' by the insertion of a full-length, and close fitting, tube of smaller diameter – watch out for this one. More serious rusting is likely to occur in the chassis outriggers and boot floor – both faults repairable at a cost. We have all heard people say that aluminium bodies do not corrode – this is simply not true. Very serious erosion of aluminium can, and does, occur when it is in contact with a ferrous metal such as steel. This is a chemical reaction which happens in the presence of a suitable fluid acting as an electrolyte – impure water will do. Check the alloy body carefully as thin gauge alloy sheet is very difficult, and therefore expensive, to repair.

Mechanically, Cobras are very robust and there is no serious parts problem as the majority of components came from mass-production cars. The relevant owners clubs are the best source of information on the parts that are difficult to obtain.

By far the biggest headache

for the buyer will be that of determining an individual car's originality, although again the owners' clubs may be able to help with specifications relating to individual chassis numbers. The most important thing here is that the modifications incorporated into an individual car consist of genuine Shelby American optional equipment. It is *essential,* when talking real Cobra money, that the car can be identified as an original production unit: there are a number of cars around built from spares and major components of written-off cars which are passed off as genuine Cobras ... beware. Unfortunately, with competition cars it is almost inevitable that they will have been subjected to major modifications and rebuilds, which will not have been documented. With these cars you are on your own.

Copy Cobras

The Cobra is probably the world's most copied car. Ever since the original car's demise, lookalikes and kit cars of varying quality have been available from a host of manufacturers. The number of imitations is hardly surprising, however, when the small number of originals, and their current value, is taken into account. And, after all, imitation *is* the sincerest form of flattery.

Beribo Replica Automobiles. This company run by John Berry and Peter Ibbotson produces the B.R.A. Cobra kit. The body is in high-quality glass fibre (the original moulds having been taken from a 289 Cobra) supported on a square-section steel chassis of B.R.A.s own construction. All suspension, and most driveline components should be taken from a donor MGB – including engine/gearbox for the basic model. The Rover 3.5-litre V8 can also be used, and, when fitted with Holley carb, Offenhauser manifolds, pancake filter and tubular exhaust, pumps out 220bhp – giving the car performance almost identical with the 289 Cobra. Kit prices are very reasonable.

Fibreglass-body 'Cobra' kits are also available in the UK from **Cheetah Cars** (Cheetah Cobra, Ford Cortina-based) and, **Unique Autokraft** (Python Roadster, Jag XJ-based).

In North American replica Cobras, ready for the road, are available from Aurora and ERA Repica Automobiles (in the latter case a small amount of finishing is necessary). The ERA car, based on the Cobra 427, has a fibreglass body mounted on chassis and suspension of ERA's manufacture. Engine is Ford's 427 V8. The Aurora Mk II is manufactured in Canada as a complete car with fibreglass body – it is based on the

289 Cobra. Power comes from a modern Ford 302cid V8. Both these cars are fairly expensive; at around the same price you could buy a real Cobra.

Also in North America, both the Butler Cobra and the Contemporary Classic Motor Car Co Cobra, can be bought in kit form. Again both cars are fibreglass-bodied and utilise their manufacturer's own chassis frames. Suspension for the CCMC car is courtesy of the Jaguar E-type, whilst power is provided by a Ford

427 V8 – if you can find one. The Butler car uses suspension/steering components from Jaguar, MGB and Camaro, and is powered by a *Chevrolet* V8 complete with automatic transmission. Both kit cars, based on the 427 Cobra, are realistically priced.

CLUBS, SPECIALISTS & BOOKS

Clubs

If you own a Cobra, are thinking of buying one or are just an enthusiast of the model, you are strongly advised to join the relevant club. Not only will you find yourself amongst like-minded enthusiasts, you will also find that a club can offer very real help in the provision of information and location of parts. Often it is also possible to obtain useful discounts through club membership.

H. Baker, **AC Owners Club**, Tudor House, Manor Road, Great Bowden, Market Harborough, Leicester, England.

Shelby American Automobile Club, 22 Olmstead Road, West Reading, CT 06896, USA.

Specialists

The following is a small selection. Contact with one of the owners' clubs will produce many more names and addresses.

AC Cars Ltd, Summer Road, Thames Ditton, Surrey KT7 0RD, England.

C.P. Autokraft, Brooklands Industrial Park, Weybridge, Surrey, England. (Formerly called Cobra Parts and now the builders of the AC Mk IV 'Cobra').

Nostalgia, Briar Forge, Vicarage Causeway, Hertford Heath, Hertfordshire SG13 7RT, England, (0992 58891/51093). Rod Leach's Nostalgia is Europe's leading specialist Cobra dealer.

Shelby/Tiger/Cobra Parts & Restoration, 3099 Carter Drive, Kennesaw, Ga 30144, USA. (404-427 0020).

Cobra Automotive Specialties, PO Box 3726, Amity Station, New Haven, Ct 06525, USA.

Shelby Parts & Restoration, 2215 O'Connor Road, Green Bay, Wisconsin 54303, USA. (414-434 3645).

Cobras Ltd, Rt 5,387 Sutton Road, Barrington, Illinois 60010, USA (312-381 1133).

Lookalikes/kit cars are available from:

Beribo Replica Automobiles, Wheatley Hills Garage, Thorne Road, Doncaster, South Yorkshire, DN2 5AL England. (0302 23325).

D.J. Sportscars, 2 Edinburgh Place, Edinburgh Way, Harlow Essex, England. (0279 442661/2).

Cheetah Cars, Unit 20, Stella Gill Ind. Est., Chester-le-Street, Co Durham.

Unique Autocraft, 3 South Road, Templefields, Harlow, Essex, CM20 2AP England. (0279 412794).

Metaline Ltd, 73 Cavendish Meads, Ascot, Berkshire, England. (0990 26603).

Aurora, Richmond Hill, Ontario, Canada.

ERA Replica Automobiles, 608-612 East Main Street, New Britain, Ct 06051, USA. (203-229 7968).

Contemporary Classic Motor Car Co Inc, 5-7 Tecumseh Avenue, Mt Vernon, NY 10553, USA. (914-664 8906).

Butler Racing Inc, 11811 Major Street, Culver City, CA 90203, USA (213-391 1785).

Books, etc ...

Shelby American Guide by Richard J. Kopec. Published by Shelby American Automobile Club.

Carroll Shelby's The Cobra Story by Carroll Shelby and John Bentley. Published by Motorbooks International.

AC by Martyn Watkins. Published by Foulis/Haynes.

Carroll Shelby's Racing Cobra by Dave Friedman and John Christy. published by Newport Press /Osprey.

AC & Cobra by John McLellan. published by Dalton Watson.

Ford Cobra Guide by Bill Carroll. published by Sports Car Press. (Believed to be out of print).

Readers may also be interested to note that the Cobra was the subject of an American hit record. *Hey Little Cobra,* and that Bill Cosby gives an account of his supercharged 427 Cobra on his comedy record *200 mph.*

PHOTO GALLERY

1

2

3

1. The bare facts. Skeletal chassis and superstructure of the coil-spring type Cobra. This chassis is the ex-Bill Cosby 'CSX 3303' as rebuilt by Brian Angliss. It was to become the second of the three cars owned by Rod Leach to bear the COB 1 registration. (Photo courtesy of Nostalgia)

2 & 3. More chassis detail. These close-ups of the front (2) and rear (3) of a 427 chassis show how the same basic chassis as the original leaf-spring cars was adapted to carry coil-spring independent suspension front and rear. Of particular note in the rear suspension are the visible rose-type joints which made the geometry completely adjustable. Rack and pinion-type steering became standard after the first 100-120 Mk II cars. (Photos courtesy of John McLellan)

4

5

6

4. This close-up of front suspension of a late leaf-spring car illustrates detail differences, particularly how one half of the transverse spring acted as the top suspension arm on each side.

5 & 6. Although taken from opposite sides of the chassis these comparative pictures of 289 leaf spring (5) and 427 coil-spring (6) rear brake assemblies illustrate important differences. Note in particular the drive pegs on the hub of the 427 – with this system it is essential to wire the ears of the spinner after tightening. In the 289 picture the additional caliper for the handbrake can be clearly seen. (Photo 6 courtesy of Nostalgia)

7 & 8. An interesting comparison between chassis plates. The plate on the British-built car gives the prefix 'COB' whilst that of the car finished in America has the prefix 'CSX' believed to stand for 'Carroll Shelby Export'.

7

8

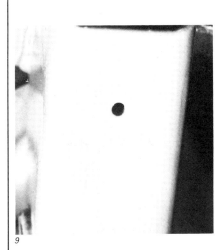

9

10

11

12

13

9. The chassis number is duplicated elsewhere on the chassis as illustrated by this close-up of the coil-spring mount of a 427.

10, 11 & 12. Close-ups of the original badges of a European 289 (10 & 11) and the special wing/fender badge, created by a watchmaker, for COB 1 (12). (Photo 12 courtesy Nostalgia)

13 & 14. Wire wheels of an original 289 compared with the Halibrands on a 427. This particular 427 has been converted to full C/S specification and features outboard exhausts with nominal silencing ... it sounds impressive!

14

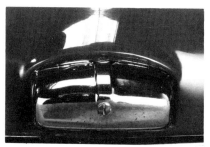

15, 16, 17, 18 & 19. Rectangular one-piece tail lamp fitted to a leaf-spring 289 compared with twin, circular rear lamps on 427 (15 & 16); Lucas number plate lamp of 289 (17); front quarter differences between 289 (18) and 427 (19) – note particularly tripode-type headlamp of 289 and its lack of air intakes. In common with many proprietary components fitted to Cobras, none of these items were fitted strictly to any one model type. Item fitment depended as much on availability as on design.

15

16

17

18

19

20

20 & 21. Details of original leaf-spring 289 front and
rear-end styling. These pictures show well the design of
egg crate type grille and front/rear tubular bumpers.

21

22, 23, 24 & 25. More details of 289 design. In these studies can be seen the boot/trunk handle (22), quick-release fuel filler cap, bonnet/hood handle and windscreen wiper, and the front wing/fender air outlet. In the latter picture can be seen the pronounced flat on the wheelarch lip. This feature, which was embodied on both Mk I and Mk II cars, became the archetypal Cobra body style.

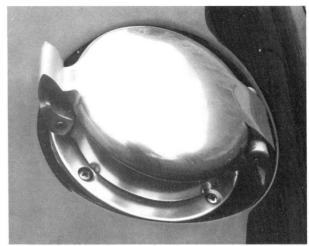

27

26

28

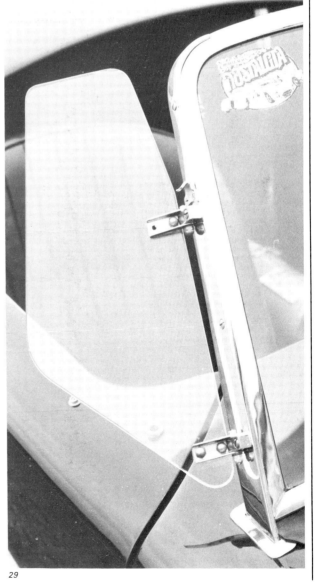

26, 27, 28 & 29. Detail cameos of 427 design. S/C-type
roll-bar (on earlier 289 competition cars the support bar
of the roll hoop ran forwards, between the seats); quick-
release, comp-type fuel filler; front wing/fender badge
and air outlet (the latter in stainless steel on this Brian
Angliss-detailed car); windscreen side wind deflector –
the etching of the word 'Cobra' being another Angliss
touch.

29

30 & 31. Single quad carburettor of 289 and twin quads of full S/C spec 427. Note the general lack of tidiness in the wiring/plumbing of these original engine compartments. (Photo 31 courtesy of Nostalgia)

30

31

32

33

34

32. A stage in the re-bodying of the ex-Bill Cosby car, chassis number CSX3303, in the UK. The important aspect of this picture is that it clearly shows the point beneath the door at which the two halves of the body are joined – correct alignment here is essential! The body has to be separated at this point before it can be removed from the chassis. (Photo courtesy of Nostalgia)

33. The totally original engine compartment of a standard 427, CSX3359. Even very recently, this car had less than 600 miles recorded on the odometer! (Photo courtesy of Nostalgia)

34. By way of contrast, the engine compartment of COB 1 during construction. Here the twin-turbos, normally covered by insulating housings, can be clearly seen. (Photo courtesy of Nostalgia)

35

36

37

35, 36, 37 & 38. Interior details. Crude door release and hinges of an original 289 (35 & 36) compared with the same items on a 427 re-trimmed by Brian Angliss.

38

39

40

41

39. The immaculate, original interior of the less-than-600-mile standard 427 which recently passed through Rod Leach's hands. You may be able to see that the odometer reads just 507 miles! (Photo courtesy Nostalgia)

40. Not much room in the rear luggage compartment of a leaf-spring 289 – and not much more in the later, wider coil-spring cars ...

41. Not much room in the fascia glovebox either, especially with the intrusion of the windscreen demister vent pipe. The map light is not standard.

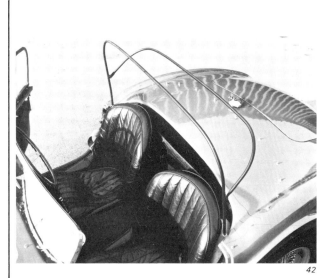

42

43

42 & 43. Raising the roof with a Cobra! Stage one, fit the hood sticks into the support tubes alongside the seats; stage two, fasten the hood fabric to the windscreen rail; stretch the fabric backwards over the frame and clip the hood to the studs around the rear deck.

44. ... or, perhaps it's easier to fit the tonneau and forget the hood!

45. The sidescreens locate in ferrules inset in the door top edges.

44

45

46

47

46. A leaf-spring 289 ready for you to drive away ...

47. A 'King' Cobra indeed! This perfect Mk II 289 once belonged to Crown Prince Saud and latterly to Prince Michael of Kent. Its standard (apart from the bonnet scoop) bodywork concealed a fully-developed Gurney-Eagle GT40 engine, with alloy heads and 4 x 48IDA Weber carburettors. The resulting 430 bhp gave considerably better performance than many 427 (7-litre) Cobras, 100 mph being attainable in about 10 seconds thus making it one of the most potent Mk IIs in the world. (Photo courtesy of Nostalgia)

48

49

48, 49, 50, 51 & 52. Five studies of the very original MkII leaf-spring 289 of John Haynes.

51

50

52

53. One of just three left-hand drive 289s built on 427-type coil-spring chassis, and in fact the very last Cobra to be built by AC Cars in England. Note that the car has the bulbous non-flared rear wheel arches which were a feature of all coil-spring 289 cars. (Photo courtesy of Nostalgia)

54. AC 289s, or MkIIIs, on the 'production line' at AC's Thames Ditton factory in 1965. These were of course coil-spring cars, and again feature the bulbous rear wheel arches which look so odd with the narrower tyres of the 289. Looking on are Sales Manager, M. G. Wright (left) and Service Manager, F. Laremore. (Photo courtesy of John McLellan)

53

54

55

56

55, 56, 57, 58 & 59. Five cameos of a beautiful 427 which, during its restoration in England by Brian Angliss, was converted to full C/S specification. Every inch of this car is immaculate, and its road performance is shattering ...

57

58

59

60. The superb, less-than-600-mile Cobra 427
previously mentioned. This car features one of the
numerous rear wheel arch designs. This style stands so
far proud of the original wheels that they look very
awkward. As a result many cars have subsequently been
fitted with wider wheels to help improve the looks.
(Photo courtesy of Nostalgia)

60

61 & 62. The Ghia-Willment 427. Bodies by Ghia of Turin, this unusual car was apparently immensely practical and trouble free – in fact it was used by a recent owner for daily commuting into London! (Photos courtesy of Nostalgia)

63 & 64. Daytona, the classic Pete Brock design which brought so much glory to the Shelby organisation. This particular car came within an ace of being imported to Britain. (Photos courtesy of Nostalgia)

61

62

63

65

66

65. One of the 1963 Le Mans Cobras pictured in 1964 at Brands Hatch for the British GP meeting, where it won the Ilford Trophy race driven by Jack Sears and entered by Willment. In this picture the car is sans the aluminium hardtop it would have sported in the classic French endurance event. However, the modified wheel-arches are evident as are the wing vents and steeply raked windscreen. (Photo courtesy of John McLellan)

66. The Sanderson/Bolton Cobra 289 coupé-style hardtop during the 1963 Le Mans race. The car, entered by AC, swept on to take 7th overall and 4th in GT class – not bad for a newcomer in the world's toughest endurance race ... (Photo courtesy of John McLellan/Autocar)

67

68

67. One of the five FIA Roadsters built with the 1964 GT Championship in mind. This car is pictured at the 1964 Nürburgring round, where it was driven by Schlesser/Attwood. (Photo courtesy of John McLellan/Ford Motor Company)

68. The Schlesser/Grant Daytona at Le Mans in 1965; unfortunately the car retired with mechanical problems. By this time the writing was on the wall for the Daytonas, as Ford wanted 'their' GT40 to be the standard bearer for the future. (Photo courtesy John McLellan)

69

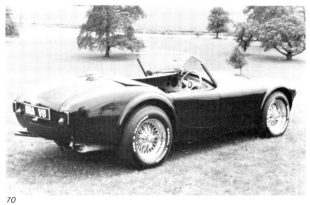

70

71

72

69. The Willment Cobra Coupé at a Silverstone race for historic cars, driven by current owner Baron de Rothschild. This car was the Willment team's interpretation of the Daytona and, built in 1964, was based on an ex-roadster chassis. The car was much used in British events and often for international endurance races. (Photo courtesy John McLellan/Graham Murrell)

70, 71 & 72. Three of the Cobras copy cars currently available. The Beribo 'B.R.A. 289' (70); the Unique Autocraft 'Python Roadster' (71); the Era Replica Automobiles 'E.R.A. 427SC'. See text for more information and addresses. (Photos courtesy of manufacturers)

73

73. Perhaps the finest of the Cobra copy cars, the AC Mk IV built by Autokraft at Weybridge.

74. The interior of the AC Mk IV showing clearly the luxurious interior, so very different from the original Cobra philosophy.

74

1

C1, C2 & C3. Three shots illustrating well the simple and timeless lines of the AC Shelby Cobra Mk II 289. This right-hand drive car, chassis number COB6029, was built in the UK in 1964 and registered on January 1, 1965. The car is currently owned by John Haynes. Whilst not by any means in concours condition, this Cobra is very original right down to its un-retouched paintwork and period wing mirrors.

2

3

*C4, C5 & C6. A different kettle of snakes altogether!
76 COB, chassis number CSX3210, is a genuine Shelby
AC Cobra 427 which was brought to Britain from the
USA in the mid-seventies. Whilst not a great deal is
known about the car's early history, since its arrival in
the UK it has received much attention from Cobra-
specialist, Brian Angliss. During the total restoration of
this car it was brought up to full C/S specification and
was the subject of much detailing – for instance, the
inner wings are in stainless steel and the quality of the
interior re-trimming is faultless, more than can be said
for original Cobras! At the time it was photographed, at
Haileybury School, Hertford Heath, the car was in the
process of being sold to an American musician by Rod
Leach, and was soon to head west, across the Atlantic.*

4

5

6

C7 & C8. This Cobra really is venomous! Rod Leach's COB 1, the world's ultimate Cobra ... and resident in the UK. This car, chassis COB6131, has a fascinating history. Carroll Shelby built a pair of twin-supercharged 427s, one of which he retained for his personal use, the other going to comedian Bill Cosby. The latter car was crashed by a subsequent owner and the remains of its body and chassis found their way back to the UK under the ownership of Rod Leach – the dual supercharged engine stayed in the USA. Whilst CSX3303 (the Cosby car) was undergoing restoration and conversion to right-hand drive by Brian Angliss he was simultaneously working on his own pet Cobra project. Brian had acquired an original Cobra chassis, COB6131, which had been used to mount the replica vintage body of a car which featured in the film 'Monte Carlo or Bust', and was busily creating his own 'Ultimate Cobra'. The superstructure of the original coil-spring chassis had been widened by four inches and was also three inches longer and would have featured an out-and-out racing 7-litre engine had he not run out of spare time to complete the project. Rod saw the potential of the Angliss Cobra and was able to acquire the partly completed project by selling the ex-Cosby car, which by now had been rebuilt to 427 C/S specification. The story continues in the caption for C16 ... (Photos courtesy of Nostalgia)

7

8

10

9

11

C9, C10, C11 & C12. The 'offices' of a 289 (C9 & C12),
a 427 as re-trimmed by Autokraft (C10) and the twin-
turbo COB 1 also trimmed by Autokraft (C11). Note the
boost gauge, top left, of COB 1 and the Hurst shifters
fitted to both 427s. The 289 has a comfortable, well-
used feel and shows accurately, warts and all, the
quality of finish in an original standard Cobra. All of
these cars have manual transmission, although some
thirty 289s and four 427s were built with automatic
transmission.

12

C13, C14 & C15. Three Cobra engine compartments. The first picture (C13) shows a standard 289 engine with single quad carburettor; next (C14) is the engine of 427 Cobra, chassis number CSX3210, which has been converted to full C/S specification; lastly (C15) the engine of the Cobra registered 750 HOT, one of not more than three UK 427 Cobras to feature Weber carburation. (Photo courtesy of Nostalgia)

13

14

15

16

17

18

C16. The story continues from caption C7 & C8 ... Having acquired the Angliss-modified chassis/body Rod Leach was himself determined to create the ultimate Cobra. However, he was worried about the tractability for road use of the highly tuned 427 engine which was then fitted to the car. Having owned the ex-Cosby car, what could have been more natural for Rod than to use forced induction for power and driveability? Thus, it was decided to build a 427 engine with twin turbo-chargers, and the resulting power plant shown here pumps out in the region of 700bhp on full song! The engine is fitted with a single Holley 850cfm carburettor and a Holman and Moody medium-rise 427 running a compression ratio of 6.8:1. (Photo courtesy of Nostalgia)

C17 & C18. Compare the width of a 289 leaf-spring car with that of a coil-spring 427. It probably looks more here, but the difference is in fact just 7-inches. The 427 features a roll bar, which is correct for this car's C/S specification.

C19. The locking wire running from spinner to wheel is essential on Cobras with peg-drive hubs. The wheel arch protector in stainless steel is not a standard feature, but is an invaluable aid to protecting a Cobra's paintwork.

C20. The date is March 22, 1984 and the moment is historic. Five of the, at most, eight 7-litre Cobras then in Britain congregate at Rod Leach's premises in Hertford Heath, Herts: an event unlikely to be repeated as several of these cars have now left the country. The Weber carburated engine of the car in the foreground is shown in picture C15. (Photo courtesy of Nostalgia)

19

20

C21. One of the two 289 Cobras with hardtops, built for the 1963 Le Mans race by AC Cars. This car was also entered by AC Cars and was driven to 7th place overall by Sanderson/Bolton. The other Cobra failed to finish. These cars were innovative in many areas, as detailed in the text. (Photo courtesy of L.A.T.)

C22. The FIA Roadster of Masten Gregory against a typical Targa Florio backdrop during the 1964 event. (Photo courtesy of L.A.T.)

21

22